慧

著鄺

如

緣

Chinese Characters

Their Art and Wisdom

Rose Quong

DOVER PUBLICATIONS, INC.
Mineola, New York

Bibliographical Note

This Dover edition, first published in 2007, is an unabridged republication of the work originally published by Pantheon Books, Inc., New York, in 1944 under the title *Chinese Wit, Wisdom, and Written Characters.*

Library of Congress Cataloging-in-Publication Data

Guang, Rusi.
  [Chinese wit, wisdom, and written characters]
  Chinese characters : their art and wisdom / Rose Quong.
    p. cm.
  Originally published: Chinese wit, wisdom, and written characters. New York : Pantheon Books, 1944.
  ISBN 0-486-45434-7 (pbk.)
  1. Chinese language—Writing. I. Title.

PL1171.G83 2007
495.1'11—dc22

2006052103

Manufactured in the United States of America
Dover Publications, Inc., 31 East 2nd Street, Mineola, N.Y. 11501

TO

DR. KINN WEI SHAW

WHO FOSTERED

THIS LITTLE BOOK

AND WHOSE CALLIGRAPHY

ADORNS ITS PAGES

Chinese written characters reveal not only thought processes of the Chinese mind, but of the universal human mind. As pictures, which the greater number originally were, they have universal appeal.

Throughout the Far East, practically, Chinese characters or symbols are known, however much the spoken languages vary. The symbols, for example, 人 *man and* 天 *heaven are as commonly known as the symbols 1 and 2 are in the West.*

The forms 人 *and* 天 *are written with the modern pen. The same characters written with the Chinese brush show the rhythm and flow of "life-movement", which a good calligrapher ever seeks to capture on paper. "Life-movement" is the first essential in Chinese art, and calligraphy is peculiarly the national art of China.*

With changes in writing instruments and materials came changes of form - rounded characters were squared and curved strokes made angular. Also, when characters were combined, they were modified to blend more harmoniously into an organic whole. Forms altered too, as styles of writing varied from period to period. The liveliest imagination, therefore, is often required to find in a character a likeness to the original.

Characters are grouped under key-characters known as "radicals" which, in composition, give a clue to meaning. Characters giving a clue to sound are known as "phonetics"; although these relate specifically to sound, possible meanings are here suggested as aids for remembering the characters.

Characters do not change to denote singular or plural. There are no declensions or conjugations in Chinese. The character 人 *means "man" and "men", and the picture of an eye on two legs* 見 *means "to see", "seeing", "saw", etc.*

Only one or two of many meanings are given for each character, the chief aim being to show how thought and form have combined to make of the Chinese written character-further than a symbol of meaning-an expression of philosophy, as well as of art.

APPROXIMATE PRONUNCIATION

	As in		As in
a	far	ien	alien
ai	aisle	ir	shirk
ao	how	o	or
ei	eight	ou	soul
en	sun	u	rule
erh	her	un	put
ia	yard	ü	ee [with pursed lips]

TONES

Each character is a monosyllable spoken in one or other of the following four tones:

		Marked	As in	
1st	even [rather high pitch]	–	counting	"1, 2, 3 stars"
2nd	rising	/	a question	"Stars?"
3rd	falling-rising	∨	a question incredulously	"What! Stars?"
4th	falling	＼	a definite statement	"Yes, Stars."

The tone is part of the pronunciation, but only the emphasized word in a phrase need be given the full tone.

IN THE BEGINNING man,
standing upright on his two legs,
realizes himself a human being

A MAN; A PERSON;
A HUMAN BEING　　　　rén

Stretching out his arms, he calls
himself -

BIG　　　　dà

But overtopping man (ren),

be he ever so big (da),

there lies -

HEAVEN; THE SKY　　　　tien

Means also -

DAY
(since the sky growing light
is dawn of day)

Every day　　　　tientien

Everybody　　　　ren-rén

A big stroke

separating

two little divided ones,

makes -

shiao

SMALL

Big (da)

standing together with

little (shiao)

calls attention to -

dashiao

SIZE;
GREAT AND SMALL

Mencius (B. C. 372 - 289),
famous follower of Confucius,
said: -
" The great

man (daren)

is he who never loses the

heart (shin)

of a child."

Here is a picture of the heart which was considered to be the seat of the mind - thought and feeling germinating in the heart. You may remember it as

a heart

indicating three beats

THE HEART;

THE MIND

shin

Man (ren)

when doing something with great care, concentrates his mind (shin) to such a point that he scarcely breathes; with less breath the heart (shin)

expands less, i. e. remains small (shiao).

Hence-

CAREFUL;

TAKE CARE

shiaoshin

L a o - t s e (b. B. C. 604), with Confucius, a moulder of the Chinese heart and

mind (shin),

said:- "Begin difficult things while they are easy; do great things while they are small. The difficult things of the world must once have been easy; the great things must once have been small.

. . . . A thousand-mile journey begins with one step."

In the beginning, with the tiniest first step-

shiăoshin  *TAKE CARE!*

THE SUN AND THE MOON

In the

sky (tien),

pouring light and warmth upon

the whole world, shines the sun,

now written-

THE SUN;
DAY
(beginning at sunrise)

rìr

And at night, shedding the
beauty of her silvery light upon

the whole world, shines the moon

now written -

THE MOON
MONTH
(beginning at new moon)

yüèh

Nothing could shine as bril-
liantly as these two heavenly

lights, so man combined the sun

and the moon

for the idea of–

ming

BRILLIANT;
BRIGHT;
ENLIGHTENED

L a o t s e said: "He who knows others is clever; he who knows himself is

enlightened (ming)."

The name of the brilliant Ming dynasty A.D. 1368-1644, became known to the western world mainly through the fine porcelains of that period.

The sky grows light when

the sun (rir)

just peeps above the horizon.

A tiny stroke gives the idea of "peeping above the horizon."
Hence the symbol for–

bái

CLEAR;
WHITE;
PLAIN

Anything that is

bright (ming)

and clear (bai)

to man, he understands.

明
白

TO UNDERSTAND;
UNDERSTOOD; &c

明
白

mingbai

At times, however, one feels
somewhat like a bird
fluttering upward, but not
getting beyond

a fixed limit

不

This may remind you of a
negative -

一

NOT

不

bù

I don't (bu)

understand (ming)

(bai)

不
明
白

bùmingbai

In asking a question, offer the
two alternatives

míngbai —
bùmíngbai

明
白
不
明
白

Do you understand?   *i. e.*

Understand (ming)

    (bai)

or not (bu)

understand (ming)

    (bai)

Dark clouds come and go, but there is always the blue sky; and beyond the darkest night there is always the dawn.

In the "Book of Changes", some 3000 years old, is rooted the belief: "When a thing reaches its limit, it turns around."

So, ever hopefully, man anticipates the morrow as

a bright (ming)

day (tien)

Hence -

míngtien

TOMORROW

MAN AND WOMAN

Man's first work was to till the field. With its furrows, here is depicted –

A FIELD

tien

Daily toil strengthened his muscles. A picture of man's muscle represents –

STRENGTH; FORCE

leè

A field

where man puts forth his

strength

is the symbol for –

MALE; MASCULINE

nán

One day man opened his

eyes

mù

Now written –

EYE

And he saw not only with his
eyes, but with his heart and
mind. He became

one big eye

on two legs,

jièn

TO SEE; SEEING; SAW, &c.

For here was a human being

with gently-curving breasts

Now written –

nǚ

WOMAN;
FEMININE

nánren

Man

nǚren

Woman

Man (nanren),

in his strength and brilliance,

is as the

sun (rìr)

Woman (nǚren)

in her gentleness and beauty,
is as the

moon (yueh).

Both shining, in turn, at their
proper times.

Man conceived the idea of peace
and contentment as -

one woman

under a roof.

PEACE;
CONTENTMENT  *ān*

Three women -

ADULTERY  *jiēn*

To make his happiness
complete, woman would bear
him a

child

Now written -

dz  *CHILD*

 *In the possession of woman*

and child

man found his greatest good. Hence -

hao  *GOOD*

  "One hundred men (nanren)

can make an encampment;

one woman (nüren)

can make a home."

haobuhao   *Is it good?*   *(hao)*

Will that do?   *(bu)*

Are you well?   *(hao)*

STILL MOUNTAINS AND
FLOWING WATER

A time for work and a time for
rest - so man's years ripen.
In nature he

sees (jien)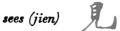

the rhythmic pattern - movement
and rest.

Mountains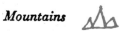

now written -

MOUNTAINS  shan

in their grandeur and serenity,
manifest strength born of
stillness.
L a o t s e said: "Who can
make the muddy water clear?
Let it be still, and it will clear
itself."

Rippling water now written –

shwei 水

WATER

in its ebb and flow, manifests strength born of movement. "Nothing so gentle, so adaptable, as

水 *water (shwei),*

yet it can wear away that which is hardest and strongest."
– Laotse.

Nature's rhythm – movement and rest – is symbolised in every Chinese landscape painting by

 mountains (shan)

and water (shwei)

never one without the other.
Hence –

shanshwei  *Landscape;*

*Throughout the universe all
things flow in orderly succession.*

ONE	一	*ēe*
TWO	二	*èrh*
THREE	三	*sān*

*And the year advances
regularly towards its end, to
begin its cycle over again.*

JANUARY	一月	*ēe-yüeh*
FEBRUARY	二月	*érh-yüeh*
MARCH	三月	*sān-yüeh*

*Movement and rest - neither
should exceed nor fall short*

Here is depicted a pair of

scales.

兩

Combine with scales

"*two*"

*for the idea of repetition.
Hence –*

dzài *AGAIN;
REPEATED;
A SECOND TIME*

*The rhythm of life – activity
and rest – going and returning.*

dzàijien Good-bye

míngtien-iien  *See you tomorrow!*

THE CLEAN-SWEPT
HEART

A tree expresses itself through
its leaves; man expresses
himself through his deeds.

With its branches.

trunk,

and roots,

here is -

A TREE;
WOOD

mù

"One tree does not make a
forest."

A FOREST;
A GROVE

lín

DENSE;
THICK WITH TREES

shēn

Man plucked with his hand

two leafy branches

Man's hand with its
five fingers
is now written –

shou **HAND**

Combined with other characters,

one form of hand

holding something,

becomes
Two leafy branches depicted as

brushwood,

held in the hand,

represents –

hwèe **A BROOM**

Put a broom

over the heart

When the heart is swept clean,
wit and wisdom flourish.

This may call to mind –

hwèe **WIT;**
WISDOM

"Man combs his hair very morning; why not his heart?"

Without wisdom (hwee)

man wants everything in his

own hands (shou)

He even reaches for the

moon (yueh)

In combination with other

characters, a simplified form of

hand

is written-

With his hand

on the moon,

man dreams of having the ten

thousand things he desires.

This may remind you of-

HAVING; TO HAVE; &c

means also-

THERE IS; THERE ARE: &c

yeou

The ancients wrote hand over meat

After a thousand-odd years "meat" came to look like the "moon", so that by A. D. 100 a famous Chinese dictionary containing some 10,000 characters, and which is still in use, classified this character under "moon" instead of "meat"

To have (yeou)

has ever since appeared as if a hand were reaching for the moon instead of laying hold of meat.

"Every blade of grass has its drop of dew."

yeoushwei

There is water   (yeou)

(shwei)

TOWARDS PROSPERITY

*Man's hopes have ever been for
an Ideal Rule under which
would exist peace and plenty.*

For shelter and security,

a roof,

and under it piled high,

the products

of his field.

**ABUNDANCE;
PROSPERITY;
TO ENRICH**

fù

Confucius (B. C. 551-479)

said: "First enrich (fu)

the people, then teach them."

*In order to nourish life, man
must be able to lay his*

hand (shou)

on food.

Strips of dried meat

wrapped up

is now written -

ru

MEAT;
FLESH

A combining form is simplified to

which looks like the moon.

Anciently when a pupil first appeared before his teacher, he always presented an offering. The humblest offering was a

little dried meat wrapped up

Confucius said: "Upwards from the man bringing his bundle of dried meat for my teaching, I have never refused instruction to anyone." From this, a teacher's salary came to be called "dried-meat money".

This picture represents the

horns, legs and tail of a sheep -

now written –

A SHEEP 　羊 　yáng

Mutton (yang) 羊肉 　yángru

(ru)

To be able to obtain food, man
had to have a weapon of some
kind. This is –

A SPEAR 　戈 　ḡo

When in his hand

man holds a spear, 手戈

then easily emerges the big "I".

I; ME 　我 　wo

I have sheep (wo) 我有羊 wo-yeou-yáng

(yeou)

(yang)

The aggressive "I", with

spear in hand, 我

is subdued and grows gentle as

a sheep 　羊

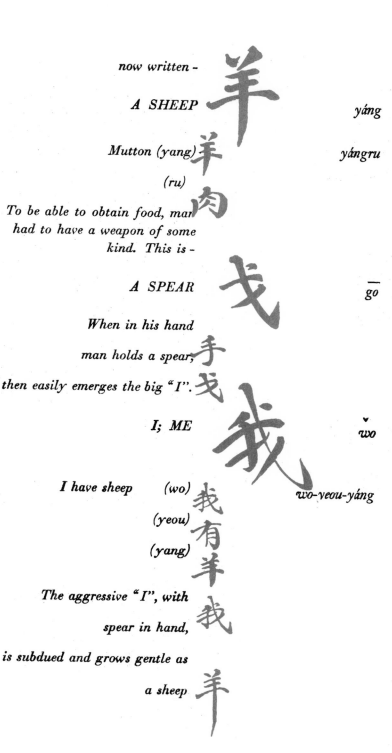

èe

when justice and righteousness prevail.
Hence –

JUSTICE;
RIGHTEOUSNESS;
RIGHT CONDUCT

Ageless wisdom associates the element of metal sword, spear, etc. with the human quality of justice.

The real "I"

stands with a protecting sword or spear of justice beside "you"

another human being (written thus in combination)

as beside a little one

in need of shelter.

This may help you to remember –

nee

YOU

nee-yeou-yángru

You have mutton	*(nee)*
	(yeou)
	(yang)
	(ru)

ELDER BROTHER SPEAKS

Two layers of earth

from which growing things

sprout

represents –

THE EARTH

ˇ
tu

Two men

sitting upon the earth

is the symbol for –

TO SIT; SITTING; SAT, &c.

ˋ
dzo

When two men sit together they open their

mouths

now written –

THE MOUTH

ˇ
kou

And from their mouths stream

sound-waves,

which become –

yén **WORDS**

The man of greater knowledge and experience speaks to the other as to a younger brother.

He becomes a big mouth of authority

on two legs

and calls himself –

shīung *ELDER BROTHER; A SENIOR*

Here is a sign which gives an idea of

separating

Elder brother

clearly separating

his words,

means -

TO SPEAK;
TO SAY; SAID; &c  shwo

A plant blossoming from the

earth

suggests the idea of growth,
of life.
Hence -

TO PRODUCE;
TO BE BORN; sheng
BIRTH;
LIFE; &c

This character, without the

middle stroke,

written

and placed on two legs,

stresses the idea of adavncing.
It is the symbol for -

IN FRONT;
FIRST; shien
BEFORE

先　　He who is

生　　the first (shien)

　　　born (sheng),

　　　i. e. the elder, is worthy of
　　　respect.
　　　Therefore –

shīen-sheng　先　　Teacher;
　　　　　　Sir;
　　　　　　Mr.

生

　　　In China old age has always
　　　been revered.
　　　"A family that has an old
　　　person in it has a jewel."

shīensheng-hǎo　先　　How are you, sir?　(shien)

生　　　　　　　　(sheng)

好　　　　　　　　(hao)

haohǎo　好　Very well.　(hao)

好　　　　　　(hao)

NATURE'S COLOR

The sun warms into green

plants growing from the earth.

In the early alchemist's stove

minerals glowed into color.
The green of plants, the blue
of the sky, the blue-green of
the sea - nature's color, first
of all colors - is written:

GREEN;
BLUE;
BLUE-GREEN

$ch\bar{i}ng$

The pleasing and inviting

sound of "ching"

added to

a word

makes -

PLEASE;
TO INVITE

$ch\check{i}ng$

chǐngchǐng

Please help yourself;
After you

Man liked the idea that by
nature

woman's

mouth

should assent to his wishes.
Hence -

rú

LIKE; AS;
EQUAL TO

One man

is like

another in that he has

a heart

responsive to pain and
pleasure.   His own feelings
guide him as to the feelings of
others.   Hence -

shù

RECIPROCITY;
TO FORGIVE

Confucius, when asked whether
there was one word which
could serve as a rule of
practice for the whole of one's
life, replied: "Is not

reciprocity (shu)

such a word? What you
would not want done to
yourself, do not do to others."

The picture of a two-leaved
door means -

A DOOR; *mén*
A GATEWAY

A mouth

at the door

means -

TO ASK; *wèn*
TO INQUIRE

May I ask   *(ching)*   *chingwèn*
Will you please tell me (wen)

This is an ear
now written -

erh

AN EAR

An ear
at the door
means -

wén

TO HEAR

erh-wén	"The ear (erh)
bùru	hearing (wen)
mu-jièn	is not (bu)
	equal to (ru)
	the eye (mu)
	seeing." (jien)

chingdzò	Please take a seat.	(ching)
		(dzo)

ching

Please - after you

PRECIOUS COWRIES

*Long ages ago, throughout the
world, man treasured cowries.*

This is a cowrie,

showing feelers.

Now written -

COWRIES;
VALUABLES

bèi

And this is a net

for fishing, or holding things.

Combining form written

*In a very early China cowrie
shells were used as money.
Man went to market with*

his net

and cowries.

Hence -

TO BUY;
BOUGHT; &c

mǎi

A plant produced from the ground,

that is a product put forth

to net

cowries

is the symbol for –

mài

TO SELL;
SELLING; &c

maĭmaĭ

Trade;
Buying and selling

Two spears

destroying the value of

cowries,

makes –

CHEAP;
WORTHLESS;
HUMBLE

jièn

A basket
of precious cowries
is -

EXPENSIVE;
PRIZED;
HONORABLE

Big (da)
emphasized by
a tiny stroke
becomes -

EXCESSIVE;
TOO

Too expensive (tai)

(gwei)

Madam; Mrs. (tai)

(tai)

Man
born
of woman

gwèi

tài

taigwèi

tàitai

has a name. In a remote era the family line was traced through the mother. Hence -

shing 姓

A SURNAME

The Book of Family Names of the Chinese people, compiled in the Sung dynasty (A. D. 960-1127), contains between 400 and 500 names.
One of these names is

林 *Lin*

meaning forest.
In Chinese the surname precedes the personal name and title, as in any directory of names.

Lin-taitai 林太太 Mrs. Lin   (Lin)

(tai)

(tai)

What is your name?

gweishing 貴姓 i. e. Honorable (gwei)

name?   (shing)

My name is Lin.

jienshingLin 賤姓林 Humble   (jien)

name   (shing)

Lin   (Lin)

EAST AND WEST

At break of day through

the trees

man saw the rising of

the sun.

Hence -

EAST

  $\overline{dung}$

At sunset birds seek their nests.
This was once the picture of a
bird on its nest;
it means -

WEST

  $\overline{shee}$

A sage born in the east   (dung)

a sage born in the west   (shee)

though they be thousands of
miles apart, though they be
separated by thousands of years,
when their principles are put
into practice, it is like the
fitting together of the two
halves of a tally.-
(Book of Mencius)

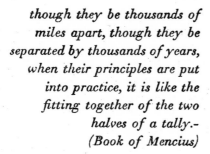

The East   (dung)

and the West   (shee)

*of a broken world, meeting as
the two halves of a tally, would
verify victory of the great
harmony, universal peace.*

 A tree

with top bent over

*to suggest the bending tops of
ripe sheaves of grain, means –*

 hó    *GROWING GRAIN*

 Grain

is agreeable to

 the mouth.

Hence –

 *hó*   *AGREEABLE TO;
TO HARMONIZE WITH;
HARMONY*

tài-   *The great harmony;
Universal peace*

ho

*When of old the victor
triumphantly returned from
battle, his enthronement upon*

 a high seat of honor

was accompanied by loud
beating of drums.

A hand
with a stick
beating a drum
is now written

VICTORY

kai

All things exist between

east (dung)

and west (shee)
Hence -

THINGS;
AN ARTICLE;
EAST AND WEST

dūngshee

In the west
women
have wanted more of life
outside the home than women
in the east.   This is suggested
as a reminder of -

WANTED, &c;
TO INTEND TO

yào

woyao-mai-dungshee 我要買東西

I want to buy some things;

(wo)

(yao)

(mai)

(dung)

(shee)

Three united lines of a triangle suggesting amalgamation,

and two nuggets of gold in the earth,

may remind you of -

jin 金

GOLD;
METAL

Two spears

breaking gold

into pieces, means -

chien 錢

MONEY

"With money a dragon, without money a worm."

woyao-chien 我要錢

I want some money   (wo)

(yao)

(chien)

RIGHT NAMES

Better than knowing how to
satisfy one's desires is knowing
where to stop.   An age-old
symbol of man's foot stopping,
right stroke the toes and
left stroke the heel, is now -

TO STOP;
TO HALT

止

jř

止
一

Stopping

at the exact limit

means -

EXACT;
CORRECT;
TO RECTIFY

正

jèng

The idea of taking action is in

a hand holding a rod

which later became

and is now written

To rectify

by taking action

支
攴
攵
正
攵

is –

jèng 政

TO GOVERN;
GOVERNMENT

月

*A crescent moon, with one
stroke less than*

*the moon
represents*

shèe 夕

EVENING;
DUSK

夕

*In the dusk
when man is not clearly seen,
by word of*

口

*mouth
he gives his name.
Hence –*

míng 名

NAME;
REPUTATION

*Confucius, when asked what
should be the first step in
governing a country, replied:
"Rectify   (jeng)*

jèng-míng 正名

names"   (ming)

"Let the ruler be a ruler, the minister a minister, the father a father, and the son a son." For when things no longer mean what their names indicate, then, said Confucius, "the people are confused and know not how to move hand and foot."

The sun

in its heavenly course

is exact.

Hence -

IS; ARE;
TO BE, &c.

shir

Is that so or not?   *(shir)*   shìrbushir

(bu)

(shir)

Yes, it is.   shìr

Two evenings

used to mean many evenings. In the course of centuries "evenings" vanished, but "many" remained.

MANY;
MUCH   d̄o

Very many;   *(hao)*   ˇhaodo

A good deal.   *(do)*

Footprints made by

亻

one step with the left foot

and one with the right

彳

is the symbol for

shíng

行

TO WALK;
TO TRAVEL;
TO BE PRACTICABLE;
TO WORK

Everyone to his calling;
everything to its proper use.
From the Book of Liu An,
Prince of Huai Nan (d. 122
B. C.): "Even an ugly hat
must be worn on the head."

shíngbushing

行
不
行
不
行

Will it do or not?   (shing)
Will it work?
(bu)

(shing)

bùshing

No, that won't do.   (bu)

(shing)

THE MARRIAGE SONG

The Book of Poetry, compiled by Confucius from songs of the people, opens with a marriage song welcoming the bride of King Wen (B. C. 1231-1135), and beginning with the call of a bird to its mate. Thus Confucius implied that between husband and wife is the first of human relationships, and marriage the prelude to civilized living.

A youth grown big

and reaching maturity was invested with

the cap

of manhood.

Hence -

A HUSBAND;
A DISTINGUISHED PERSON

fū

Taking hold of a person by

the ear

with one's hand

is -

TO TAKE HOLD OF;
TO SELECT

chū

取
女

To take hold of

a woman

means –

chü

TO MARRY

When a man marries, he puts

a broom

十
丑
女

into the hand

of a woman

thus bestowing upon her the rulership of the home.

Hence –

chee

A WIFE

chüchee

To marry;   *(chu)*
To take a wife

            (chee)

When a woman marries, she goes forth from the home of her parents. Plants pushing forth from the soil, is the symbol for –

chu

TO GO FORTH

Peasants, settled in a home, possess domesticated animals. Since the wild boar is the symbol of the wealth of the forest, the domesticated pig may well be the symbol of prosperity in the home.

Under a roof

a pig

now written

is the symbol for –

**A HOME;
A FAMILY**   jiā

A woman

with a home

signifies –

TO BE MARRIED   jià

A woman

going forth

to be married

means –

To get married;   (chu)
To take a husband

(jia)   chujià

Cloud-like vapor rising from the earth

resembles breath.

cheè

BREATH;
VAPOR

Another form of this character looks like

three puffs of air

breathed into something.

That which gives

breath

to the heart

and gracious motion (retarding cross-bar makes slow i. e. gracious motion)

is -

ai

LOVE

"Loving union with wife and children is like the music of lutes." (From the Book of Poetry)

wo-ainee

I love you   (wo)

           (ai)

           (nee)

SILK COCOONS

*Ages ago a Chinese Empress, in
her garden, came across a
despicable worm nibbling the
leaves of a mulberry tree. With
wonder, she watched its
transformations. Then one day
she presented the Emperor
Huang-ti (B. C. 2697) with a
silk cocoon.*

Here are two silk cocoons

with three silk threads

now written

Doubled, the character is -

SILK

*From the Empress the people
learned how to rear silk-worms
and to spin silk. Soon many
hands were busy gathering
mulberry leaves.*

Many hands

*busy among the branches of
a tree*

depicts -

A MULBERRY TREE

szï

sang

"With time and patience the mulberry tree becomes a silk gown."

Silk and bamboo were writing materials before the discovery in China of paper, accredited to Ts'ai Lun (105 A. D.).

A plant from the soil grows upward

Growing out of water many a plant lies flat

Form changed to

To be written upon, paper should like

silk

lie flat as a water-plant

Hence –

jǐr

PAPER

From only two cocoons, one could wind the finest threads. Hence –

FINE;
SMALL
Simplified to

yao

The symbol for music was once five drums (representing the five tones of the Chinese scale) upon a stand of

wood

Later the five drums
became

two small drums, or silk-
stringed lutes, on either side of
a large drum.

MUSIC

yüèh

Where music is there is joy,
hence the same symbol, but
pronounced differently,
represents -

JOY;
PLEASURE;
TO REJOICE

lò

Music brings harmony to spirit,
mind and body. The Emperor
Shen-nung (B. C. 2737)
discovered in herbs also a
harmonising influence on the
body.

This is grass or herbs

Combining form simplified to

To a body disordered

herbs

restore

harmony

Hence -

MEDICINE

yaò

Tea was one of the herbs
discovered by Shen-nung.

廿 Herbs

入 under cover

木 to dry, after being picked from

a tree-like plant, make

'cha 茶 TEA

Before writing was invented,
records were kept by means of
knotted cords of vegetable fibres.

林 Fibres stripped from the
hemp plant

广 then stored under shelter
is the symbol for –

má 麻 厶 HEMP

Adding fine

this symbol was in time
adopted as –

ma 麼 A sign of interrogation

厶 Simplified form

Have you any paper?   (nee)

neeyeou- 你 (yeou)

jirma 有 (jir)

紙 (ma)

yeou 有 Yes, I have some

BAMBOO BOOKS

When man first wrote, he held

a stylus

in his hand

and scratched a line

on a tablet

of bone or shell, bamboo or wood. About 4000 years ago this character was written -

A pen

A mouth

and in it a word

meant -

To speak

A pen

speaking

makes -

A BOOK;
WRITINGS

shu

Later, writing was brushed on silk and paper. The same brush and materials were used for painting.

The artist with his

brush

paints

a subject

Of the frame, there now remains only

the bottom side.

hwà

A PAINTING

Poetry, painting and calligraphy form the great trinity of Chinese arts.

"China's friend" - thus has been named

the bamboo

which in its flexibility and strength, yields to the storm but never breaks; and in its usefulness, does service in countless forms.
Now written –

jú

BAMBOO

Combining form

When bamboo formed the handles of

pens

the character became –

bee

A PEN

*The first books were made of
narrow bamboo slips, and
characters were written from
top to bottom, in vertical
columns, as they are still
written today. Hui Shih (4th
century B. C.), famous logician,
used to travel, it is said, with
five cartloads of bamboo books.*

*Written characters came to be
cherished as under*

a roof

a child

is cherished. Hence -

A WRITTEN CHARACTER   *dẕ*

*More than 1000 years ago the
first printed book in the world
was produced in China.*

a hand

written

pressing a seal

*formed the character for seals
used in the 3rd century B. C. to
stamp impressions on clay;
these, in time, gave way to
inked impressions on paper.
About the 8th century block
printing was invented; then in
the 11th century Pi Sheng
invented movable type.*

The same written character
covers all -

TO PRINT;
TO STAMP;
A SEAL

yin

手 *The hand*

is a key-character. Written in
various forms, it gives a clue to
some kind of action.
Even part of

十 *a hand*

means doing something.

小 *Little*

丿 *diminished by*

becomes -

shao

LESS

shaojièn-
shaojièn

*I've seen little of you; i. e.
I've missed seeing you;*

少 *Less (shao)*

見 *seen (jien)*

少 *less (shao)*

見 *seen (jien)*

*As the wheel of life moves on,
man learns that by adjusting
himself to change, through
change he progresses.*

This is a chameleon

*which easily changes its color.
Hence -*

eè

CHANGES;
EASY

Imagine this as

warp threads

on a loom

As silk threads

*are woven into precious and
enduring fabrics, so wisdom is
woven into the precious and
enduring classics.   Hence -*

A CLASSIC

jīng

The oldest Chinese Classic is -

*The Book of Changes i. e.
the Changes (ee)*

eè-jing

Classic (jing)

*In transliteration, known as the
I Ching or the Yi King.*

*When Confucius lived, the
classics were written on bamboo
slips bound together with
leathern thongs*

like this

*According to the great historian,
Ssu-ma Ch'ien (b. B. C. 145),
Confucius read his copy of the
Book of Changes so much that
the leathern thongs were thrice
worn out.*

*To gather together or to join
records*

is -

lún

TO SET IN ORDER; ORDERLY

With the key-character for man

this symbol became-

lún

HUMAN RELATIONSHIPS

*Confucius insisted
that in the five human
relationships - between
ruler and minister, father
and son, husband and wife,
brother and brother, friend and
friend - rights and responsibili-
ties be mutually observed.*

Marks of feet running

and stopping

mean to advance, and form the
key-character

In combination written

This is how the ancients drew

a head with two tufts of hair
on top

Feet

and head

advancing on the same path,
is the symbol for -

THE PATH;
THE WAY

 daò

Ages ago man travelled in
chariots and wheelbarrows.
This is -

A CHARIOT;
A WHEELBARROW

 cher̄

Here are flames of

FIRE

 hwŏ

A train is

a fire (hwo)

chariot (cher)

After travelling for centuries,
man now rides in a train.
That is, he

sits in (dzo)

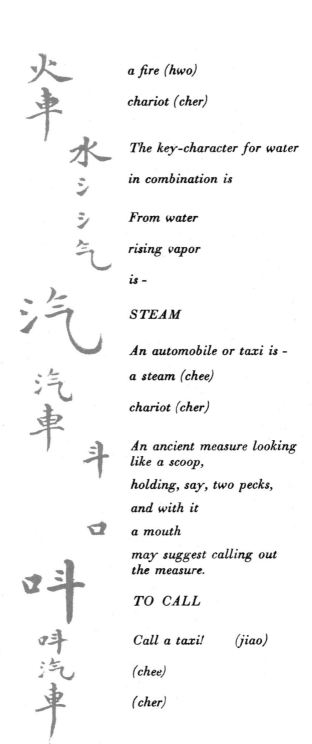

a fire (hwo)

chariot (cher)

The key-character for water

in combination is

From water

rising vapor

is -

chèe   STEAM

An automobile or taxi is -

a steam (chee)

chariot (cher)

An ancient measure looking like a scoop,

holding, say, two pecks,

and with it

a mouth

may suggest calling out the measure.

jiào   TO CALL

jiao-

chèecher   Call a taxi!   (jiao)

(chee)

(cher)

TAO

The Supreme Something that was before all created things - Laotse said he did not know Its name, but that a name might be written, he wrote -

TAO;
THE WAY,

 *dao*

All things are born af Tao and to Tao all things return as rivers flow into the sea. Tao is everywhere. It is -

ABOVE

shang

BELOW

shià

and in

THE CENTER
THE MIDDLE

 jung

of all things.

The world;   i. e. Heaven (tien)
The universe

below (shia)

Laotse's aim was to be in harmony with TAO, and at home in the universe.

Man

and two

is the symbol of all humane feeling between man and his fellow-man, of all feelings which make man a human being.

SYMPATHY; LOVING-KINDNESS; HUMANITY

rén 仁

Confucius said: "He who follows the path of

仁 humanity *(ren)*

is not far from

道 *TAO*

His faith was that by practising

恕 reciprocity *(shu)*

man would attain

仁 *the perfect human virtue (ren).*

In time it came about that, among men,

一 *each one*

口 *had to defend his own land*

戈 *with weapons.*

In a well-defined boundary

口 *the symbol is -*

COUNTRY; NATION

gwó 國

A sheep

 羊

is admired for its peace-loving virtue,

especially when it is

large 大

Hence -

ADMIRABLE;
BEAUTIFUL ˇmei

In "America" the most
pronounced syllable sounds like
"mei". Hence -

AMERICA   *Beautiful (mei)* ˇmei-gwo

Country (gwo)

Grass

and an open space

with a man in the middle

suggests a man in a jungle.
Hence -

BRAVE;

HEROIC ‾ying

In "England" the first syllable
sounds like "ying". Hence -

ENGLAND   *Brave (ying)* ‾ying-gwo

Country (gwo)

CHINA is   *the Middle (jung)* ‾jung-gwo

Country (gwo)

nee-shir

meigwo-ren

你
是
美
國
人

You are an American. (nee)

(shir)

(mei)

(gwo)

(ren)

A justly balanced figure, equal and freely expanding on both sides, is the symbol for -

p'ing

平

**PEACE;
JUST;
EQUAL**

tien-shià

ee-jia

天
下
一
家

Confucius said: "*All under Heaven, one family.*" (tien)

(shia)

(ee)

(jia)

When that comes true, then universal will be the greeting -

renrén

ping-an

人
人
平
安

"*Peace and contentment to all!*" (ren)

(ren)

(ping)

(an)

A CATALOG OF SELECTED DOVER
BOOKS IN ALL FIELDS OF INTEREST

CONCERNING THE SPIRITUAL IN ART, Wassily Kandinsky. Pioneering work by father of abstract art. Thoughts on color theory, nature of art. Analysis of earlier masters. 12 illustrations. 80pp. of text. 5⅜ x 8½. 0-486-23411-8

CELTIC ART: The Methods of Construction, George Bain. Simple geometric techniques for making Celtic interlacements, spirals, Kells-type initials, animals, humans, etc. Over 500 illustrations. 160pp. 9 x 12. (Available in U.S. only.) 0-486-22923-8

AN ATLAS OF ANATOMY FOR ARTISTS, Fritz Schider. Most thorough reference work on art anatomy in the world. Hundreds of illustrations, including selections from works by Vesalius, Leonardo, Goya, Ingres, Michelangelo, others. 593 illustrations. 192pp. 7⅛ x 10¼. 0-486-20241-0

CELTIC HAND STROKE-BY-STROKE (Irish Half-Uncial from "The Book of Kells"): An Arthur Baker Calligraphy Manual, Arthur Baker. Complete guide to creating each letter of the alphabet in distinctive Celtic manner. Covers hand position, strokes, pens, inks, paper, more. Illustrated. 48pp. 8¼ x 11. 0-486-24336-2

EASY ORIGAMI, John Montroll. Charming collection of 32 projects (hat, cup, pelican, piano, swan, many more) specially designed for the novice origami hobbyist. Clearly illustrated easy-to-follow instructions insure that even beginning papercrafters will achieve successful results. 48pp. 8¼ x 11. 0-486-27298-2

BLOOMINGDALE'S ILLUSTRATED 1886 CATALOG: Fashions, Dry Goods and Housewares, Bloomingdale Brothers. Famed merchants' extremely rare catalog depicting about 1,700 products: clothing, housewares, firearms, dry goods, jewelry, more. Invaluable for dating, identifying vintage items. Also, copyright-free graphics for artists, designers. Co-published with Henry Ford Museum & Greenfield Village. 160pp. 8¼ x 11. 0-486-25780-0

THE ART OF WORLDLY WISDOM, Baltasar Gracian. "Think with the few and speak with the many," "Friends are a second existence," and "Be able to forget" are among this 1637 volume's 300 pithy maxims. A perfect source of mental and spiritual refreshment, it can be opened at random and appreciated either in brief or at length. 128pp. 5⅜ x 8½. 0-486-44034-6

JOHNSON'S DICTIONARY: A Modern Selection, Samuel Johnson (E. L. McAdam and George Milne, eds.). This modern version reduces the original 1755 edition's 2,300 pages of definitions and literary examples to a more manageable length, retaining the verbal pleasure and historical curiosity of the original. 480pp. 5⁵⁄₁₆ x 8¼. 0-486-44089-3

ADVENTURES OF HUCKLEBERRY FINN, Mark Twain, Illustrated by E. W. Kemble. A work of eternal richness and complexity, a source of ongoing critical debate, and a literary landmark, Twain's 1885 masterpiece about a barefoot boy's journey of self-discovery has enthralled readers around the world. This handsome clothbound reproduction of the first edition features all 174 of the original black-and-white illustrations. 368pp. 5⅜ x 8½. 0-486-44322-1

STICKLEY CRAFTSMAN FURNITURE CATALOGS, Gustav Stickley and L. & J. G. Stickley. Beautiful, functional furniture in two authentic catalogs from 1910. 594 illustrations, including 277 photos, show settles, rockers, armchairs, reclining chairs, bookcases, desks, tables. 183pp. 6½ x 9¼. 0-486-23838-5

AMERICAN LOCOMOTIVES IN HISTORIC PHOTOGRAPHS: 1858 to 1949, Ron Ziel (ed.). A rare collection of 126 meticulously detailed official photographs, called "builder portraits," of American locomotives that majestically chronicle the rise of steam locomotive power in America. Introduction. Detailed captions. xi+ 129pp. 9 x 12. 0-486-27393-8

AMERICA'S LIGHTHOUSES: An Illustrated History, Francis Ross Holland, Jr. Delightfully written, profusely illustrated fact-filled survey of over 200 American lighthouses since 1716. History, anecdotes, technological advances, more. 240pp. 8 x 10¾. 0-486-25576-X

TOWARDS A NEW ARCHITECTURE, Le Corbusier. Pioneering manifesto by founder of "International School." Technical and aesthetic theories, views of industry, economics, relation of form to function, "mass-production split" and much more. Profusely illustrated. 320pp. 6⅛ x 9¼. (Available in U.S. only.) 0-486-25023-7

HOW THE OTHER HALF LIVES, Jacob Riis. Famous journalistic record, exposing poverty and degradation of New York slums around 1900, by major social reformer. 100 striking and influential photographs. 233pp. 10 x 7⅞. 0-486-22012-5

FRUIT KEY AND TWIG KEY TO TREES AND SHRUBS, William M. Harlow. One of the handiest and most widely used identification aids. Fruit key covers 120 deciduous and evergreen species; twig key 160 deciduous species. Easily used. Over 300 photographs. 126pp. 5⅜ x 8½. 0-486-20511-8

COMMON BIRD SONGS, Dr. Donald J. Borror. Songs of 60 most common U.S. birds: robins, sparrows, cardinals, bluejays, finches, more–arranged in order of increasing complexity. Up to 9 variations of songs of each species.
Cassette and manual 0-486-99911-4

ORCHIDS AS HOUSE PLANTS, Rebecca Tyson Northen. Grow cattleyas and many other kinds of orchids–in a window, in a case, or under artificial light. 63 illustrations. 148pp. 5⅜ x 8½. 0-486-23261-1

MONSTER MAZES, Dave Phillips. Masterful mazes at four levels of difficulty. Avoid deadly perils and evil creatures to find magical treasures. Solutions for all 32 exciting illustrated puzzles. 48pp. 8¼ x 11. 0-486-26005-4

MOZART'S DON GIOVANNI (DOVER OPERA LIBRETTO SERIES), Wolfgang Amadeus Mozart. Introduced and translated by Ellen H. Bleiler. Standard Italian libretto, with complete English translation. Convenient and thoroughly portable–an ideal companion for reading along with a recording or the performance itself. Introduction. List of characters. Plot summary. 121pp. 5¼ x 8½. 0-486-24944-1

FRANK LLOYD WRIGHT'S DANA HOUSE, Donald Hoffmann. Pictorial essay of residential masterpiece with over 160 interior and exterior photos, plans, elevations, sketches and studies. 128pp. 9¼ x 10¾. 0-486-29120-0

THE CLARINET AND CLARINET PLAYING, David Pino. Lively, comprehensive work features suggestions about technique, musicianship, and musical interpretation, as well as guidelines for teaching, making your own reeds, and preparing for public performance. Includes an intriguing look at clarinet history. "A godsend," *The Clarinet,* Journal of the International Clarinet Society. Appendixes. 7 illus. 320pp. 5⅜ x 8½. 0-486-40270-3

HOLLYWOOD GLAMOR PORTRAITS, John Kobal (ed.). 145 photos from 1926-49. Harlow, Gable, Bogart, Bacall; 94 stars in all. Full background on photographers, technical aspects. 160pp. 8⅜ x 11¼. 0-486-23352-9

THE RAVEN AND OTHER FAVORITE POEMS, Edgar Allan Poe. Over 40 of the author's most memorable poems: "The Bells," "Ulalume," "Israfel," "To Helen," "The Conqueror Worm," "Eldorado," "Annabel Lee," many more. Alphabetic lists of titles and first lines. 64pp. 5$^{3}/_{16}$ x 8¼. 0-486-26685-0

PERSONAL MEMOIRS OF U. S. GRANT, Ulysses Simpson Grant. Intelligent, deeply moving firsthand account of Civil War campaigns, considered by many the finest military memoirs ever written. Includes letters, historic photographs, maps and more. 528pp. 6⅛ x 9¼. 0-486-28587-1

ANCIENT EGYPTIAN MATERIALS AND INDUSTRIES, A. Lucas and J. Harris. Fascinating, comprehensive, thoroughly documented text describes this ancient civilization's vast resources and the processes that incorporated them in daily life, including the use of animal products, building materials, cosmetics, perfumes and incense, fibers, glazed ware, glass and its manufacture, materials used in the mummification process, and much more. 544pp. 6⅛ x 9¼. (Available in U.S. only.) 0-486-40446-3

RUSSIAN STORIES/RUSSKIE RASSKAZY: A Dual-Language Book, edited by Gleb Struve. Twelve tales by such masters as Chekhov, Tolstoy, Dostoevsky, Pushkin, others. Excellent word-for-word English translations on facing pages, plus teaching and study aids, Russian/English vocabulary, biographical/critical introductions, more. 416pp. 5⅜ x 8½. 0-486-26244-8

PHILADELPHIA THEN AND NOW: 60 Sites Photographed in the Past and Present, Kenneth Finkel and Susan Oyama. Rare photographs of City Hall, Logan Square, Independence Hall, Betsy Ross House, other landmarks juxtaposed with contemporary views. Captures changing face of historic city. Introduction. Captions. 128pp. 8¼ x 11. 0-486-25790-8

NORTH AMERICAN INDIAN LIFE: Customs and Traditions of 23 Tribes, Elsie Clews Parsons (ed.). 27 fictionalized essays by noted anthropologists examine religion, customs, government, additional facets of life among the Winnebago, Crow, Zuni, Eskimo, other tribes. 480pp. 6⅛ x 9¼. 0-486-27377-6

TECHNICAL MANUAL AND DICTIONARY OF CLASSICAL BALLET, Gail Grant. Defines, explains, comments on steps, movements, poses and concepts. 15-page pictorial section. Basic book for student, viewer. 127pp. 5⅜ x 8½. 0-486-21843-0

THE MALE AND FEMALE FIGURE IN MOTION: 60 Classic Photographic Sequences, Eadweard Muybridge. 60 true-action photographs of men and women walking, running, climbing, bending, turning, etc., reproduced from rare 19th-century masterpiece. vi + 121pp. 9 x 12. 0-486-24745-7

CATALOG OF DOVER BOOKS

ANIMALS: 1,419 Copyright-Free Illustrations of Mammals, Birds, Fish, Insects, etc., Jim Harter (ed.). Clear wood engravings present, in extremely lifelike poses, over 1,000 species of animals. One of the most extensive pictorial sourcebooks of its kind. Captions. Index. 284pp. 9 x 12.   0-486-23766-4

1001 QUESTIONS ANSWERED ABOUT THE SEASHORE, N. J. Berrill and Jacquelyn Berrill. Queries answered about dolphins, sea snails, sponges, starfish, fishes, shore birds, many others. Covers appearance, breeding, growth, feeding, much more. 305pp. 5¼ x 8¼.   0-486-23366-9

ATTRACTING BIRDS TO YOUR YARD, William J. Weber. Easy-to-follow guide offers advice on how to attract the greatest diversity of birds: birdhouses, feeders, water and waterers, much more. 96pp. 5³⁄₁₆ x 8¼.   0-486-28927-3

MEDICINAL AND OTHER USES OF NORTH AMERICAN PLANTS: A Historical Survey with Special Reference to the Eastern Indian Tribes, Charlotte Erichsen-Brown. Chronological historical citations document 500 years of usage of plants, trees, shrubs native to eastern Canada, northeastern U.S. Also complete identifying information. 343 illustrations. 544pp. 6½ x 9¼.   0-486-25951-X

STORYBOOK MAZES, Dave Phillips. 23 stories and mazes on two-page spreads: Wizard of Oz, Treasure Island, Robin Hood, etc. Solutions. 64pp. 8¼ x 11.   0-486-23628-5

AMERICAN NEGRO SONGS: 230 Folk Songs and Spirituals, Religious and Secular, John W. Work. This authoritative study traces the African influences of songs sung and played by black Americans at work, in church, and as entertainment. The author discusses the lyric significance of such songs as "Swing Low, Sweet Chariot," "John Henry," and others and offers the words and music for 230 songs. Bibliography. Index of Song Titles. 272pp. 6½ x 9¼.   0-486-40271-1

MOVIE-STAR PORTRAITS OF THE FORTIES, John Kobal (ed.). 163 glamor, studio photos of 106 stars of the 1940s: Rita Hayworth, Ava Gardner, Marlon Brando, Clark Gable, many more. 176pp. 8⅜ x 11¼.   0-486-23546-7

YEKL and THE IMPORTED BRIDEGROOM AND OTHER STORIES OF YIDDISH NEW YORK, Abraham Cahan. Film Hester Street based on *Yekl* (1896). Novel, other stories among first about Jewish immigrants on N.Y.'s East Side. 240pp. 5⅜ x 8½.   0-486-22427-9

SELECTED POEMS, Walt Whitman. Generous sampling from *Leaves of Grass.* Twenty-four poems include "I Hear America Singing," "Song of the Open Road," "I Sing the Body Electric," "When Lilacs Last in the Dooryard Bloom'd," "O Captain! My Captain!"—all reprinted from an authoritative edition. Lists of titles and first lines. 128pp. 5³⁄₁₆ x 8¼.   0-486-26878-0

SONGS OF EXPERIENCE: Facsimile Reproduction with 26 Plates in Full Color, William Blake. 26 full-color plates from a rare 1826 edition. Includes "The Tyger," "London," "Holy Thursday," and other poems. Printed text of poems. 48pp. 5¼ x 7.   0-486-24636-1

THE BEST TALES OF HOFFMANN, E. T. A. Hoffmann. 10 of Hoffmann's most important stories: "Nutcracker and the King of Mice," "The Golden Flowerpot," etc. 458pp. 5⅜ x 8½.   0-486-21793-0

THE BOOK OF TEA, Kakuzo Okakura. Minor classic of the Orient: entertaining, charming explanation, interpretation of traditional Japanese culture in terms of tea ceremony. 94pp. 5⅜ x 8½.   0-486-20070-1

FRENCH STORIES/CONTES FRANÇAIS: A Dual-Language Book, Wallace Fowlie. Ten stories by French masters, Voltaire to Camus: "Micromegas" by Voltaire; "The Atheist's Mass" by Balzac; "Minuet" by de Maupassant; "The Guest" by Camus, six more. Excellent English translations on facing pages. Also French-English vocabulary list, exercises, more. 352pp. 5⅜ x 8½.   0-486-26443-2

CHICAGO AT THE TURN OF THE CENTURY IN PHOTOGRAPHS: 122 Historic Views from the Collections of the Chicago Historical Society, Larry A. Viskochil. Rare large-format prints offer detailed views of City Hall, State Street, the Loop, Hull House, Union Station, many other landmarks, circa 1904-1913. Introduction. Captions. Maps. 144pp. 9⅜ x 12¼.   0-486-24656-6

OLD BROOKLYN IN EARLY PHOTOGRAPHS, 1865-1929, William Lee Younger. Luna Park, Gravesend race track, construction of Grand Army Plaza, moving of Hotel Brighton, etc. 157 previously unpublished photographs. 165pp. 8⅞ x 11¾.
0-486-23587-4

THE MYTHS OF THE NORTH AMERICAN INDIANS, Lewis Spence. Rich anthology of the myths and legends of the Algonquins, Iroquois, Pawnees and Sioux, prefaced by an extensive historical and ethnological commentary. 36 illustrations. 480pp. 5⅜ x 8½.   0-486-25967-6

AN ENCYCLOPEDIA OF BATTLES: Accounts of Over 1,560 Battles from 1479 B.C. to the Present, David Eggenberger. Essential details of every major battle in recorded history from the first battle of Megiddo in 1479 B.C. to Grenada in 1984. List of Battle Maps. New Appendix covering the years 1967-1984. Index. 99 illustrations. 544pp. 6½ x 9¼.   0-486-24913-1

SAILING ALONE AROUND THE WORLD, Captain Joshua Slocum. First man to sail around the world, alone, in small boat. One of great feats of seamanship told in delightful manner. 67 illustrations. 294pp. 5⅜ x 8½.   0-486-20326-3

ANARCHISM AND OTHER ESSAYS, Emma Goldman. Powerful, penetrating, prophetic essays on direct action, role of minorities, prison reform, puritan hypocrisy, violence, etc. 271pp. 5⅜ x 8½.   0-486-22484-8

MYTHS OF THE HINDUS AND BUDDHISTS, Ananda K. Coomaraswamy and Sister Nivedita. Great stories of the epics; deeds of Krishna, Shiva, taken from puranas, Vedas, folk tales; etc. 32 illustrations. 400pp. 5⅜ x 8½.   0-486-21759-0

MY BONDAGE AND MY FREEDOM, Frederick Douglass. Born a slave, Douglass became outspoken force in antislavery movement. The best of Douglass' autobiographies. Graphic description of slave life. 464pp. 5⅜ x 8½.   0-486-22457-0

FOLLOWING THE EQUATOR: A Journey Around the World, Mark Twain. Fascinating humorous account of 1897 voyage to Hawaii, Australia, India, New Zealand, etc. Ironic, bemused reports on peoples, customs, climate, flora and fauna, politics, much more. 197 illustrations. 720pp. 5⅜ x 8½.   0-486-26113-1

THE PEOPLE CALLED SHAKERS, Edward D. Andrews. Definitive study of Shakers: origins, beliefs, practices, dances, social organization, furniture and crafts, etc. 33 illustrations. 351pp. 5⅜ x 8½.   0-486-21081-2

THE MYTHS OF GREECE AND ROME, H. A. Guerber. A classic of mythology, generously illustrated, long prized for its simple, graphic, accurate retelling of the principal myths of Greece and Rome, and for its commentary on their origins and significance. With 64 illustrations by Michelangelo, Raphael, Titian, Rubens, Canova, Bernini and others. 480pp. 5⅜ x 8½.   0-486-27584-1

CATALOG OF DOVER BOOKS

LIGHT AND SHADE: A Classic Approach to Three-Dimensional Drawing, Mrs. Mary P. Merrifield. Handy reference clearly demonstrates principles of light and shade by revealing effects of common daylight, sunshine, and candle or artificial light on geometrical solids. 13 plates. 64pp. 5⅜ x 8½. 0-486-44143-1

ASTROLOGY AND ASTRONOMY: A Pictorial Archive of Signs and Symbols, Ernst and Johanna Lehner. Treasure trove of stories, lore, and myth, accompanied by more than 300 rare illustrations of planets, the Milky Way, signs of the zodiac, comets, meteors, and other astronomical phenomena. 192pp. 8⅜ x 11. 0-486-43981-X

JEWELRY MAKING: Techniques for Metal, Tim McCreight. Easy-to-follow instructions and carefully executed illustrations describe tools and techniques, use of gems and enamels, wire inlay, casting, and other topics. 72 line illustrations and diagrams. 176pp. 8¼ x 10⅞. 0-486-44043-5

MAKING BIRDHOUSES: Easy and Advanced Projects, Gladstone Califf. Easy-to-follow instructions include diagrams for everything from a one-room house for bluebirds to a forty-two-room structure for purple martins. 56 plates; 4 figures. 80pp. 8¾ x 6⅜. 0-486-44183-0

LITTLE BOOK OF LOG CABINS: How to Build and Furnish Them, William S. Wicks. Handy how-to manual, with instructions and illustrations for building cabins in the Adirondack style, fireplaces, stairways, furniture, beamed ceilings, and more. 102 line drawings. 96pp. 8¾ x 6⅜. 0-486-44259-4

THE SEASONS OF AMERICA PAST, Eric Sloane. From "sugaring time" and strawberry picking to Indian summer and fall harvest, a whole year's activities described in charming prose and enhanced with 79 of the author's own illustrations. 160pp. 8¼ x 11. 0-486-44220-9

THE METROPOLIS OF TOMORROW, Hugh Ferriss. Generous, prophetic vision of the metropolis of the future, as perceived in 1929. Powerful illustrations of towering structures, wide avenues, and rooftop parks–all features in many of today's modern cities. 59 illustrations. 144pp. 8¼ x 11. 0-486-43727-2

THE PATH TO ROME, Hilaire Belloc. This 1902 memoir abounds in lively vignettes from a vanished time, recounting a pilgrimage on foot across the Alps and Apennines in order to "see all Europe which the Christian Faith has saved." 77 of the author's original line drawings complement his sparkling prose. 272pp. 5⅜ x 8½. 0-486-44001-X

THE HISTORY OF RASSELAS: Prince of Abissinia, Samuel Johnson. Distinguished English writer attacks eighteenth-century optimism and man's unrealistic estimates of what life has to offer. 112pp. 5⅜ x 8½. 0-486-44094-X

A VOYAGE TO ARCTURUS, David Lindsay. A brilliant flight of pure fancy, where wild creatures crowd the fantastic landscape and demented torturers dominate victims with their bizarre mental powers. 272pp. 5⅜ x 8½. 0-486-44198-9

Paperbound unless otherwise indicated. Available at your book dealer, online at **www.doverpublications.com**, or by writing to Dept. GI, Dover Publications, Inc., 31 East 2nd Street, Mineola, NY 11501. For current price information or for free catalogs (please indicate field of interest), write to Dover Publications or log on to **www.doverpublications.com** and see every Dover book in print. Dover publishes more than 500 books each year on science, elementary and advanced mathematics, biology, music, art, literary history, social sciences, and other areas.